Quiz number 4837

If The Waters Could Talk...

Written by Stuart A. Kallen

Illustrated by Kristen Copham

Published by Abdo & Daughters, 6535 Cecilia Circle, Edina, Minnesota 55439.

Library bound edition distributed by Rockbottom Books, Pentagon Tower, P.O. Box 36036, Minneapolis, Minnesota 55435.

Edited by Julie Berg

Library of Congress Cataloging-in-Publication Data

Kallen, Stuart A., 1955-
    If the waters could talk / written by Stuart A. Kallen; [edited by Julie Berg].
       p.   cm. -- (Target Earth)
    Summary: An easy-to-read introduction to the importance of water.
    ISBN 1-56239-186-0 (lib. bdg.)
    1. Water -- Juvenile literature.   [1. Water.]   I. Berg, Julie.
II. Title.   III. Series.
GB662.3.K35   1993
553.7 -- dc20   93-18953
                                      CIP
                                      AC

 Thanks To The Trees From Which This Recycled Paper Was First Made.

Abdo & Daughters
Minneapolis

They would say...

Take a walk up the creek with a talking river. Babble along

with a brook. The whispering water has much to tell. If

you listen you can hear the ocean roar.

ave you ever stood by a babbling brook? Listened to a whispering river? Heard the ocean roar? If you have, then you know that water can talk!

Creeks sing, rain pitter-patters and clouds thunder. Clouds are made of water, too! Water is noisy stuff, and I am the loudest water of all. I am the ocean.

No matter where you live, the rain that falls outside your window flows into me—the ocean! That's because water always runs downhill. Always!

'll bet you never saw water flow up! If that happened, the ceiling would get mighty wet when you took a bath.

The same thing that pulls you to the ground when you jump off a fence pulls water downhill. It's called *gravity*.

now that melts on the highest mountaintop trickles down into tiny brooks. Rain that falls does the same. As the water flows, it takes tiny pieces of the brook bed with it. That makes the brook grow larger, ever so slowly.

Many brooks are so little that you can jump over them. As the water runs down to the sea, plants and animals and humans drink some of it. But the water just keeps flowing.

Down and down the water goes. Dozens of brooks flow into one creek. Gravity keeps pulling the water down to the ocean. Just as dozens of brooks flow into a creek, dozens of creeks flow into a stream.

Sometimes the water stops its journey at a pond or a lake. But the water is only resting. Soon the water must run into a river.

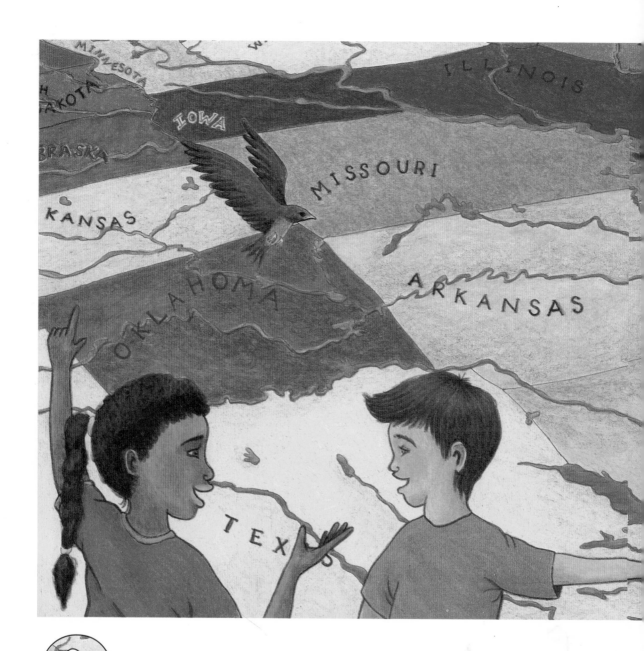

One of the biggest rivers on Earth is the Mississippi River in the United States. The Mississippi starts as a tiny stream in Minnesota. Thousands of miles later in Lousiana, the river is several miles wide. That's a big river!

When the Mississippi meets the ocean at the Gulf of Mexico, the muddy mouth of the river is called a *delta*. What started out as a few drops has turned into a mighty river.

ouses, farms, towns and cities are built on the sides of streams, creeks, and rivers.

People throw things into the river that are not water. But like the water, they flow downhill to the sea.

When it rains, weed killers that farmers spray on crops run into the river. Sometimes, when people drain their sinks and bathtubs, the soapy water runs into the river.

When oil leaks out of cars, it runs into the river when it rains. Factories use hundreds of chemicals that are dumped into the river. All of these things cause *pollution*.

People build *dams* along the rivers and streams. Dams use the power of the water to turn *turbines* which make electricity. When you turn on a light, the electricity that lights the room might be coming from river power.

Sometimes a river flows over a cliff. This is called a waterfall.

Millions of animals live in brooks, creeks, streams, rivers and oceans. We know fish live in water. But tiny little plants called *algae* also live in water. Algae are so little that you have to look through a microscope to see them.

Beavers cut down trees and build their houses in rivers. Frogs live on the edge of streams. If it weren't for rivers, there would be no life on Earth. Every living thing needs water to live.

f all the planets that we know about in our solar system, only Earth has water. And only Earth has life.

As a matter of fact, the human body is over ninety percent water. You are a walking, talking, body of water!

Eco – **A**ctivities

1 Watch a show on public television (PBS) about streams, rivers, oceans, and water pollution. Look at a listing of television shows, like the TV Guide, and find a show you think you might like. Pay close attention to the parts of the show that talk about water pollution.

2 Walk in the rain! Put on a raincoat and rubber boots and go outside when it is raining. Notice how the water flows downhill. Stick you tongue out and taste the rain. Collect rainwater in a jar and wash your hair with it later. Watch for birds, animals, and insects. Do they act differently in the rain? If you have a tape recorder, record the sound of the rain from an open window. Make sure the tape deck stays dry. Write a poem or a story about the rain. CAUTION: Only go outside in a gentle rain. Do not go outside during a lightning storm or high wind.

3 Take a walk by a stream, river, lake, or ocean. Notice how smaller streams flow into bigger ones. Does the water look clean? Do you see any pollution flowing into the water?

E~co~ – F~acts~

SAVE THE RAIN - Power plants and cars send the pollution that causes acid rain into the air. Acid rain pollutes rivers, lakes, steams, and the ocean. Ask your parents to drive less. Turn off lights when you're not in the room. Use less electricity.

TURN OFF THE TAP - Water is precious, don't waste it. Don't keep the water running when you brush your teeth. Leaky faucets waste lots of water, up to 50 gallons a day. Leaky faucets are cheap to fix. Ask your parents to fix leaky faucets in your home. A library book will show them how to do it. It's fun and easy!

WASTE NOT - Patrol a stream bank with your parents and pick up all the trash you can find. Make sure you put the trash in a trash can, or bring a garbage bag with you and take it back to your house to throw away.

Glossary

Acid rain - Rain polluted with chemicals that come from car exhaust and factories. When it falls to Earth as rain and snow, it can kill trees and pollute rivers.

Algae - Tiny, one-celled or many-celled plants that live in water. Small fish and other water animals live on algae.

Dams - Structures built across rivers, mainly to provide electricity. Dams destroy the natural river ecology.

Delta - The broad, sandy, muddy area at the mouth of a river.

Gravity - The force that pulls all things down toward the center of the Earth.

Pollution - Dirt and chemical poison on the land or in the air and water.

Turbines - Fanned wheels that are turned by water or steam to generate electricity or power.

Write or Call

Adopt - a - Stream
P.O. Box 5558
Everett, WA 98206
206-388-3313

Clean Water Action Project
1320 - 18th St. NW
Washington, DC 20036
202-457-1286

Freshwater Foundation
2500 Shadywood Road
P.O. Box 90
Navarre, MN 55392

Water Information Network
P.O. Box 909
Ashland, OR 97520
800-533-6714

TARGET EARTH™ COMMITMENT

At Target, we're committed to the environment. We show this commitment not only through our own internal efforts but also through the programs we sponsor in the communities where we do business.

Our commitment to children and the environment began when we became the Founding International Sponsor for Kids for Saving Earth, a non-profit environmental organization for kids. We helped launch the program in 1989 and supported its growth to three-quarters of a million club members in just three years.

Our commitment to children's environmental education led to the development of an environmental curriculum called Target Earth™, aimed at getting kids involved in their education and in their world.

In addition, we worked with Abdo & Daughters Publishing to develop the Target Earth™ Earthmobile, an environmental science library on wheels that can be used in libraries, or rolled from classroom to classroom.

Target believes that the children are our future and the future of our planet. Through education, they will save the world!

Minneapolis-based Target Stores is an upscale discount department store chain of 517 stores in 33 states coast-to-coast, and is the largest division of Dayton Hudson Corporation, one of the nation's leading retailers.